AMERICAN QUILTER'S SOCIETY

20TH ANNIVERSARY

CATALOGUE

of

SHOW QUILTS

Located in Paducah, Kentucky, the American Quilter's Society (AQS) is dedicated to promoting the accomplishments of today's quilters. Through its publications and events, AQS strives to honor today's quiltmakers and their work and to inspire future creativity and innovation in quiltmaking.

EDITOR: BONNIE K. BROWNING
GRAPHIC DESIGN: KAY BLACKBURN SMITH
COVER DESIGN: MICHAEL BUCKINGHAM
PHOTOGRAPHY: SUPPLIED BY THE INDIVIDUAL QUILTMAKERS

The quilt photographs in this catalog are copyrighted and may not be reproduced or used without permission of the copyright holder.

Additional copies of this book may be ordered from the American Quilter's Society, PO Box 3290, Paducah, KY 42002-3290; 800-626-5420 (orders only please); or online at www.AQSquilt.com. For all other inquiries, call 270-898-7903.

Printed and Bound in the United States of America.

The American Quilter's Society is celebrating its 20th show in 2004. Celebrating the past and honoring people who have made significant contributions is important. It is great to enjoy successes and forget failures.

But it is even more important to look to the future. Dreams for the future energize us for the present and keep us moving through changes. The quilt industry is no different than life; change is always necessary.

AQS is making a number of show rules changes for our 2005 AQS Quilt Show and Contest. The new rules are in this book and I think you'll like them. Look them over before you begin your quilt. Don't let change stop you because change is often what makes success possible. I'm looking forward to including your quilt in this book next year.

Let's celebrate the past as we look forward to the future.

Meredith Schroeder

Meredith Schroeder
AQS President and Founder

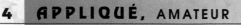

Adapted from Art Nouveau design by Alphonse Mucha.

Friendship Garden by Mabeth Oxenreider, Great American Quilts 1999, Oxmoor House

MUCHA LEAF FALL, 65" x 91", CONNIE AYERS, BREMERTON, WA.

Honorable Mention

101 102

POPPY LOVE, 86" x 93", CAROL GODREAU, BRISTOL, CT.

LEGEND OF NAUPAKA, 81" x 95", MASAKO KANDA, NAKAHARA, KAWASAKI, JAPAN.

103 104

FLOWER ARRANGEMENT, 66" x 82", KAZUMI MAKABE, SHINJUKU, TOKYO, JAPAN.

KILAKILA HALEAKALA, 81" x 103", MIDORI NAGATANI, GOTENBA, JAPAN.

| 105 | 106 |
| 107 | 108 |

ROSE SAMPLER SUPREME, 84" x 100", MARSHA D. RADTKE, FAIRFIELD GLADE, TN.

A RICH MAN'S KUKUI NUT, 82" x 114", YOKO SAKAGUCHI, SETAGAYA, TOKYO, JAPAN.

DAY LILY BASKET, 90" x 108", POLLY SEPULVADO, MD, ROSEBURG, OR.

Treasures in the Trunk: Quilts of the Oregon Trail by Mary Bywater Cross, Rutledge Hill Press; and Applique Pattern Book Vol. II by Barb Bolesta

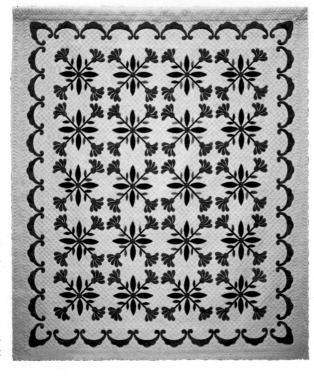

HONEYSUCKLE, 86" x 100", DIANE SHAFER-DAVIS, SEQUIM, WA.

PASSION'S FLOWERS, 86" x 86", SHELLY ABDEL-KHADER, CALLAO, MO.

109 110
201 202

SWEET ROSE LEI, 89" x 89", TOMOKO TSUNODA, SETAGAYA, TOKYO, JAPAN.

CURRANTS & CURRANTS & CURRANTS AND COCKSCOMBS, 80" x 80", MARY ANN ANDREWS, LA CANADA, CA.

Floral Ornament, Dover Publications, 1998

MAGICAL MEDALLIONS, 84" x 84", KAREN KAY BUCKLEY,
CARLISLE, PA. *Second Place*

ARABESQUE, 64" x 85", SUZANNE MARSHALL,
CLAYTON, MO. *Honorable Mention*

80 DOES IT, 81" x 97", DIANE LANE, WICHITA, KS.
First Place

FLOWER WREATH, 76" x 84", KEIKO MIYAUCHI,
NAGANO, JAPAN.
Third Place

203 204
205 206

ROSE OF KAREN, 80" x 100", IRENE MUELLER, KIRKWOOD, MO.

207 **208**
209 **210**

REMINISCENCE, 75" x 92", PHYLLIS NORTON, TOLONO, IL.

DAFFODILS, 81" x 81", EMILY PARSON, ST CHARLES, IL.

INTO HIS LIGHT, 76" x 94", PATRICIA PEPE, CRESTON, CA.

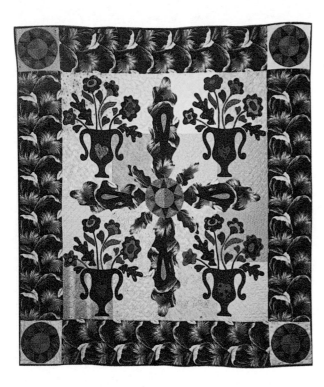

Red & Green: An Appliqué Tradition, Jeana Kimball, Martingale & Co. Inc.

LOOK WHAT I DID TO MAMA'S DRAPES, 84" x 93", JULEE PROSE, OTTUMWA, IA.

CARRIE'S VINEYARD, 90" x 90", MARILYN ROBINSON, ST. PETERS, MO.

211 212
213 214

ANNIVERSARY QUILT, 79" x 96", KAROLYN REKER, CARTERSVILLE, GA.

SPICE OF LIFE, 82" x 82", LINDA M. ROY, PITTSFIELD, MA.

Best of Show

THE FLOWER OF BUDDHIST, 80" x 81", MICHIKO SHIMA, IKOMA, NARA, JAPAN.

LeMOYNE STAR, 79" x 79", DEBRA DENSLOW, BRISTOL, CT.

215 301
302 303

STARS IN THE WEE HOURS, 80" x 100", KATHRYN A. ASH, CHICAGO, IL.

CAROLINA CLASSIC, 65" x 81", TRUDIE FAY, PHOENIX, AZ.

Third Place

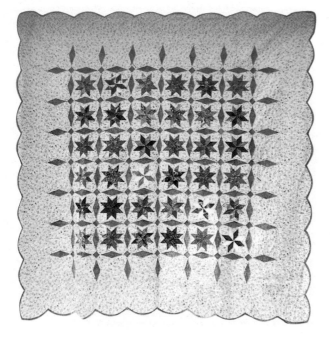

The Sun, The Moon, and The Stars 2 pattern by Linda Brannock. Star Quilt Co.

A GALAXY OF MEMORIES, 84" x 102", NANCY L. GRUENEWALD, MUSKEGO, WI.

THE ENDLESS WORLD, 74" x 86", NORIKO KIDO, NAGOYA, AICHI, JAPAN.

Second Place

304 305
306 307

First Place

IN FLOWER, 71" x 80", MITSUYO HORIUCHI, HOTAKA, NAGANO, JAPAN.

FEATHERED STAR WITH SAWTOOTH BORDER, 85" x 100", SUSAN LUERS, EVANSVILLE, WI.

Stargazey Daisiez pattern by Jan Mullen, Stargazey Quilts, North Fremantle, Western Australia

LAZY DAISY, 68" x 88", LORETTA PAINTER, NORRIS, TN.

CLIMBING MOUNTAINS, 80" x 100", LEOTA H. SCHOEDEL, ANGOLA, IN.

SQUARE PEGS, 110" x 92", VALLI SCHILLER, NAPERVILLE, IL.

FEATHERED FANCY, 90" x 90", ROSEANNE SMITH, LAWRENCE, KS.

| 308 | 309 |
| 310 | 311 |

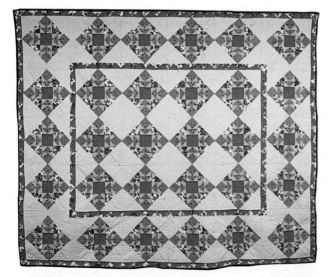

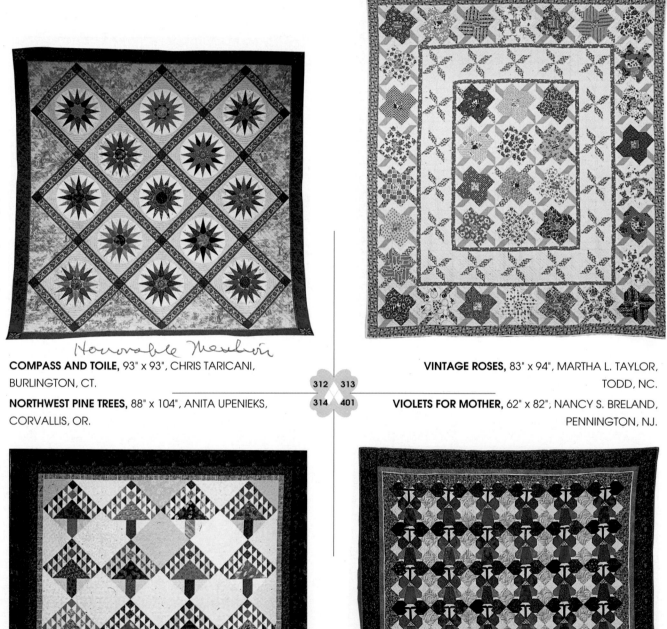

Mariner's Compass workshop with Judy Mathieson

Honorable Mention

COMPASS AND TOILE, 93" x 93", CHRIS TARICANI, BURLINGTON, CT.

NORTHWEST PINE TREES, 88" x 104", ANITA UPENIEKS, CORVALLIS, OR.

Pine Tree pattern from www.mccallsquilting.com

Bed of Roses by Anna Brandsoy, Quiltmaker, March/April 1996

VINTAGE ROSES, 83" x 94", MARTHA L. TAYLOR, TODD, NC.

VIOLETS FOR MOTHER, 62" x 82", NANCY S. BRELAND, PENNINGTON, NJ.

| 312 | 313 |
| 314 | 401 |

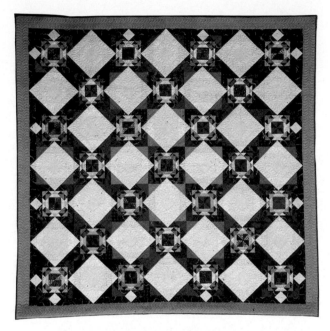

CARNIVAL STAR, 64" x 82", SUSAN K. CLEVELAND, WEST CONCORD, MN. *Second Place*

SAMPLER GONE AWRY, 65" x 85", LINDA M. FIEDLER, MEADOWS OF DAN, VA.

TENNESSEE DANCING SQUARES, 94" x 94", JUDY E. ELWOOD, MT. AIRY, MD.

IN FIELDS OF GOLD, 83" x 83", DIANE GAUDYNSKI, PEWAUKEE, WI.

| 402 | 403 |
| 404 | 405 |

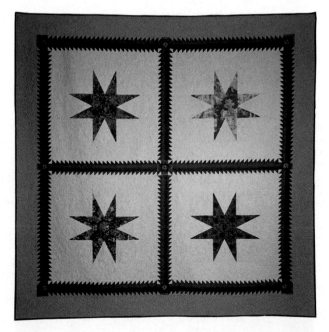

NORTH, EAST, SOUTH, WEST, AUNT SUKEY'S CHOICE IS A STAR, 97" x 97", CARLA SCHMITZ GOWER, LEWISTOWN, MO.

First Place

MARGO'S MEDALLION OF 1840, 94" x 94", CINDY VERMILLION HAMILTON, PAGOSA SPRINGS, CO.

| 406 | 407 |
| 408 | 409 |

LUCY IN THE SKY, 70" x 85", DIXIE HAYWOOD, PENSACOLA, FL.

SUNLIGHT FILTERING THROUGH THE TREES, 64" x 80", KIYOKO ISHIHARA, ASHIKAGA, TOCHIGI, JAPAN.

Judges Recognition

GETTING A ROUND TUIT, 88" x 104", LYN D. JOHNSON, COLUMBIA, SC.

PROMINENCE, 86" x 88", JUDY LAQUIDARA, OWENSBORO, KY.

410 411
412 413

TURTLE TRACKS, 82" x 82", JEAN LOHMAR, GALESBURG, IL. *Honorable Mention*

NEARLY INSANE, 90" x 92", LIZ LOIS, SALEM, WI.

New York Beauty pattern by Karen K. Stone, Dallas, TX

STAR 'N' STRIPE BEAUTY, 86" x 86", MARY MOHL, ST. LOUIS, MO.

NINE TO THE NINTH POWER, 86" x 86", SCOTT A. MURKIN, ASHEBORO, NC.

414 415

416 417

ALMOST AMISH, 71" x 80", JOANNE B. MYERS, BEND, OR.

MEGA HEXAGON, 85" x 91", HALLIE O'KELLEY, TUSCALOOSA, AL.

Country Lanes, Country Living Country Quilts, 1992, Hearst Books

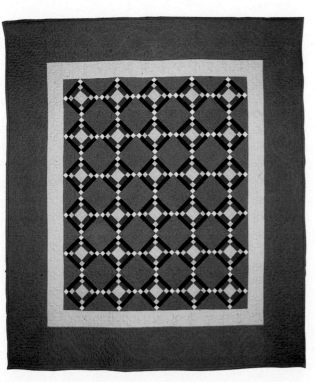

TURKISH TREASURES – A RED RENDITION, 76" x 87", BARBARA A. PERRIN, PULLMAN, MI. *Third Place*

SOMETHING NEW, SOMETHING BLUE, 94" x 110", CAROL SCHAMERLOH, BLUFFTON, IN.

| 418 | 419 |
| 420 | 421 |

FEATHERGLOW, 100" x 100", D. NADINE RUGGLES, GERLINGEN, GERMANY.

IRISH CREME, 94" x 94", CAROL A. SELEPEC, MIDLAND, PA.

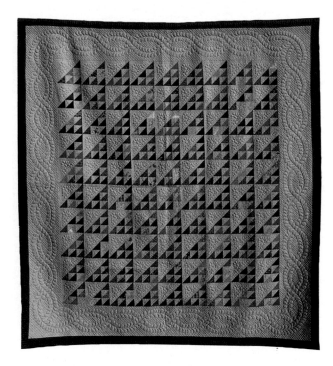

VINTAGE TREASURE, 80" x 80", MILDRED SORRELLS, MACOMB, IL.

422 **423**

BIRDS OF A FEATHER, 92" x 99", VICKI SPIERING, WAUWATOSA, WI.

501 **502**

THE TREASURES OF CHINA, 82" x 82", ANNE NELSON ANDERBERG, MARIETTA, GA. *Second Place*

WHIG'S DEFEAT, 80" x 80", CAROL G. BENSON, BARRINGTON HILLS, IL.

FIRE BLOSSOMS, 107" x 117", SERPIL BOZBAĞ, ANKARA, TURKEY.

WILD WINDING WAYS, 94" x 108", JEAN CLARK, MT. HOREB, WI.

VIEW FROM MT. DIABLO, 88" x 88", VALERIE SAUBAN CHAPLA, PLEASANT HILL, CA.

First Place

GARDEN WEDDING RING, 78" x 90", NANCY HAHN, ST. PETERS, MO.

503	504
505	506

A Garden for My Wedding Ring, a traditional pattern designed by Judy Niemeyer

Elizabethan Woods pattern by Patricia B. Campbell

Japanese Quilt Art by Setsuko Segawa; and Watercolor Impressions by Pat Maxiner Magaret & Donna Ingram Slusser, Martingale & Co., Inc.

HANNAH'S JACOBEAN, 75" x 85", JO ANN HANNAH, CLEBURNE, TX.

FLOWER FOUNTAIN, 80" x 87", HATSUNE HIRANO, HONJO, SAITAMA, JAPAN. *Third Place*

507 508
509 510

SPRING BREEZE, 75" x 85", CHIZUKO HILL, SHINAGAWA, TOKYO, JAPAN.

SHARING THE BOUNTY, 70" x 80", ANN HORTON REDWOOD VALLEY, CA.

WHAT'S IN A NAME: ROSE WINDOW TREE, 61" x 95", MICHAEL KASHEY, EDINBORO, PA.

SPRING FIELDS FULL OF POPPIES, 72" x 83", MASAKO KOTAKI, NARASHINO, CHIBA, JAPAN.

GREEN ROSES, 85" x 85", MICHIKO KONO, HOJO, EHIME, JAPAN.

HAPPY DAYS, 78" x 90", FUSAKO NAKAMURA, TOINCHO, MIE, JAPAN.

| 511 | 512 |
| 513 | 514 |

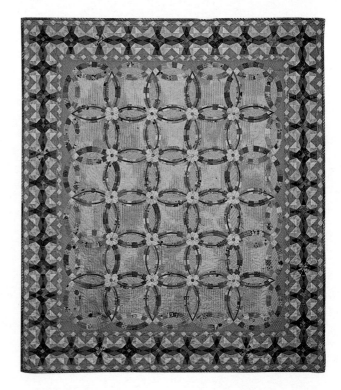

Blocks by Jinny Beyer, Elly Sienkiewicz, Ada Torrence, Maggie Walker, Mountain Mist®, Judy Martin, Cindy Greenslade, Marsha McCloskey.

20TH CENTURY SAMPLER, 85" x 100", BARBARA J. REYNOLDS, GANANOQUE, ONTARIO, CANADA.

515 516
517 518

HINA-MATSURI, 67" x 91", MICHIKO TANAKA, YAMATOKORIYAMA, NARA, JAPAN.

DOCTOR JEN, 90" x 110", POLLY SEPULVADO, MD, ROSEBURG, OR.

HALLOWEEN HAUNTS, 86" x 97", EILEEN VINCE, LIVONIA, MI.

Patterns from American Greeting Create-A-Card by Microsoft; Bittersweet & Kindred Spirits; American Patchwork & Quilting, August 1997; Spooky Faces & Scary Places by Sandy Gervais; Which Witch & The Who by Leslie Beck; Fiber Mosaics; Electric Quilt 4, Rob-n-Graves by Judi Robb, ©2001.

Honorable Mention

LAKE CABIN, 92" x 81, MACHIKO YAMAMOTO,
PEORIA, IL.

I SPY A BUTTERFLY, 75" x 87", ELLEN ANSON,
HUNTSVILLE, AL.

519 520
601 602

SURROUNDED BY GENTLENESS, 69" x 89", WAKAKO
YOSINAGA, YOKOHAMA, KANAGAWA, JAPAN.

ONKO CHISHIN, 85" x 87", MASAKO BABA,
SAKAI, OSAKA, JAPAN.

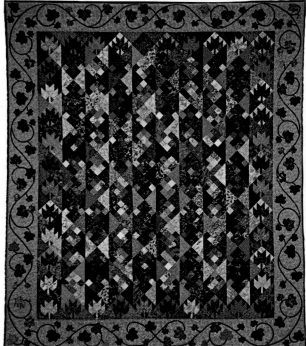

MY ROSE GARDEN, 74" x 80", SHIGEKO BABA, KASHIMA, IBARAKI, JAPAN. *Second Place*

PANGAIA, 60" x 81", BETTY COLBURN, AUSTIN, TX.

603 604
605 606

LETTERS TO SYLVIA, 73" x 86", J. PHIL BEAVER, FRENCH LICK, IN.

HIS TREES THROUGH MINE EYES, 84" x 84", SHARYN ERICKSON, BURLINGTON, WA.

Workshop with Jane Sassaman

Mariner's Compass by Judy Mathieson, C & T Publishing Inc.

Honorable Mention

THE GOLDEN CARP, 107" x 107", JANET FOGG, LAKE OSWEGO, OR.

607 **608**
609 **610**

VICTORIAN ELEGANCE, 72" x 82", JANE HOLIHAN, WALWORTH, NY. *Hand Workmanship Award*

UN PETIT COIN DE L'UNIVERS (A SMALL CORNER OF THE UNIVERSE), 86" x 96", PATRICIA MARIE HALL, KERRVILLE, TX.

CARAMBA CANASTA, 91" x 92", JANINE HOLZMAN, SITKA, AK.

LIFE, 64" x 90", KIYOKO ISHIHARA, ASHIKAGA, TOCHIGI, JAPAN.

FLOWERS FOR SCHEHEREZADE, 73" x 92", CECILIA MACIÁ, BREWSTER, MA.

611 612
613 614

AMERICAN STILL LIFE, 80" x 80", SANDRA LEICHNER, ALBANY, OR.

First Place

TUDOR ROMANCE, 66" x 80", KATHY McNEIL, MARYSVILLE, WA.

TO THE FUTURE, 70" x 82", SUMIKO MINEI, TOKYO, JAPAN.

KEEPING AUTUMN WITH ME, 93" x 93", GLADI V.
PORSCHE, LEE, NH. *Third place*

A Maze Lilies pattern by Ale Rossmann, Lotusland's

A MAZE 'N WATERLILIES, 105" x 105", RUTH OHOL,
LOCKPORT, NY.

ON MY WALK, 74" x 89", KIT ROBINSON,
PURCELLVILLE, VA.

| 615 | 616 |
| 617 | 618 |

LET THE SEEDS FALL WHERE THEY MAY, 84" x 94",
SHARON V. ROTZ, MOSINEE, WI.

SITTING BULL, 90" x 93", SHARON SCHAMBER, JENSEN, UT.

GRAVITY, 75" x 86", COLLEEN WISE, PUYALLUP, WA.

| 619 | 620 |
| 621 | 622 |

MAZE, 77" x 88", KUKIKO YAMASHITA,
MASHIKI, KUMAMOTO, JAPAN.

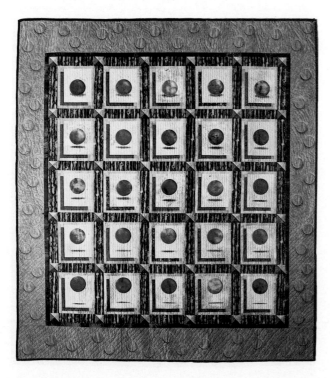

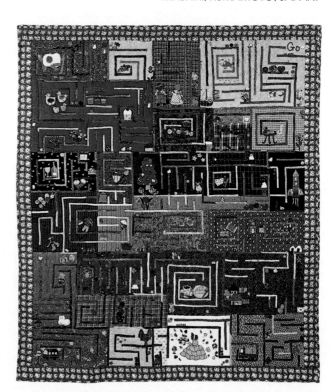

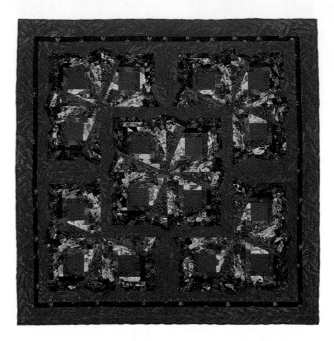

OLD GLORY, 91" x 93", JANET FOGG, LAKE OSWEGO, OR.
Second Place

SATSUMA, JANE FRENKE, 93" x 93", BERKELEY SPRINGS, WV.

701 702
703 704

FEEL THE MAY WIND, 72" x 82", MIKI GOMI,
AKIRUNO, TOKYO, JAPAN.

I STILL DREAM IN COLOR, 69" x 80", MARY L. HACKETT,
CARTERVILLE, IL.

HIS LIGHT REFLECTED, 86" x 86", RENAE HADDADIN, SANDY, UT.

ROCK STAR, 81" x 81", BARBARA OLIVER HARTMAN, FLOWER MOUND, TX. *Third Place*

PEACH BLOSSOM VALLEY, 88" x 88", BETTE HADDON, DeFUNIAK SPRINGS, FL.

THE QUILTER, 62" x 85", BETH PORTER JOHNSON, HOUSTON, TX.

705	706
707	708

DAY STAR, 80" x 87", CHRIS KLEPPE, MILWAUKEE, WI.

BEWITCHED, 68" x 80", JEANNETTE TOUSLEY MUIR, MEDFORD, NJ.

709 710
711 712

DIAMOND DUST, 84" x 84", PHILIPPA NAYLOR, DHAHRAN, SAUDI ARABIA. *First Place*

SUNSET, SUNRISE, SUNSET, 62" x 90", ELAINE PLOGMAN, CINCINNATI, OH.

Honorable Mention

COLOURS SHOWER ONTO GRENADA, 91" x 96", SABINE CIBERT, LYON, FRANCE.

BLUE BERRY SKIES, 88" x 101", KATHLEEN BADEN, KERNERSVILLE, NC, AND TERRI LARUE. QUILTED BY THERESA DEWALT.

713 714
801 802

MOONSHADOWS, 72" x 90", CAROL TAYLOR, PITTSFORD, NY.

FRIENDSHIP'S GIFT, 86" x 110", DEBRA BALLARD, MIDLAND, MI, MARY JO KERLIN, AND ELSIE VREDENBURG.

Compass Star pattern by Anne Donaghy Designs

MARK AND ELLIE'S WEDDING QUILT, 108" x 108", PAT BECKER, CHELSEA, MI, QUILTED BY SUE POLLARD & JANNA ROBERTSON.

SPIRIT OF THE DRAGON, 105" x 111", MYRLE S. BLACKWELL, CENTER, TX, QUILTED BY JANINE LAENGER.

803 804

805 806

PINEAPPLES FROM THE BERRYPATCH, 93" x 93", BERRYPATCHER'S BEE, SPARTA, MI.

GARDEN PARTY, 91" x 102", LOU ANNE P. BYARS & FRIENDS, PROSPERITY, SC.

New York Beauty pattern by Karen K. Stone, Dallas, TX

Workshop with Carol Liebzeit

Baltimore Beauties & Beyond: Studies in Classic Album Quilt Appliqué by Elly Sienkiewicz, C & T Publishing Inc.

Medallion Mystery Pattern . *New Zealand Quilter Magazine*, Issues 35-37

DREAMING OF BALTIMORE, 85" x 85", COASTAL QUILTERS GUILD, SANTA BARBARA, CA.

PIECEMAKERS TIMES & SEASONS 2002, 90" x 90", GERRY DAVIS, GRUVER, TX, QUILTED BY SUSIE MILLER.

THE SPIRIT OF NEW ZEALAND, 80" x 81", ROSEMARY CROMER, OVERLAND PARK, KS, AND MARY HIBBS.

ONLY GOD IS PERFECT, 60" x 96", DULWICH QUILTERS, LONDON, UNITED KINGDOM.

807 808
809 810

Piecemakers Times & Seasons Quilt Calendar 2002

FANS AND FLOWER BASKETS, 72" x 90", GENESEE VALLEY QUILT CLUB, INC., WALWORTH, NY.

811 | 812
813 | 814

COUNTERPOINT, 74" x 84", REGINA GROSS, SAN DIEGO, CA, AND KAY OLIVIA.

MIDNIGHT GALAXY, 80" x 90", JULIA GRABER, BROOKSVILLE, MS, QUILTED BY MATTIE MAST.

FADE TO BLACK, 82" x 92", HELEN HARDWICK, EL DORADO HILLS, CA, AND CHRYSTINE MARTIN.

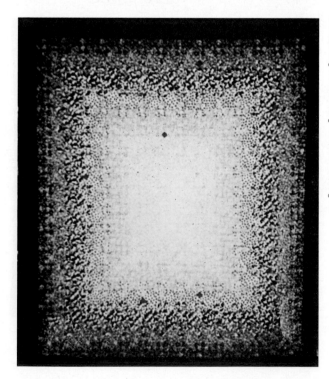

Magic Stack-n-Whack® Bethany S. Reynolds, American Quilter's Society.

Tradition With A Twist: Variations on Your Favorite Quilts by Blanche Young & Dalene Young Stone, C & T Publishing Inc.

"1492," 82" x 82", IRMA GAIL HATCHER, CONWAY, AR, PATTY GALAS, AND LINDA TAYLOR.

HERSHEL AND ISABEL, 63" x 82", JAN KEELER, INDEPENDENCE, MO, AND DENISE HESTER.

LET FREEDOM RING, 84" x 93", HONEYBEE QUILTERS, MEDINA, OH.

NEAPOLITAN, 85" x 85", JULIE KENNEDY, CLYMAN, WI, QUILTED BY JANICE L. WALSH.

815 816
817 818

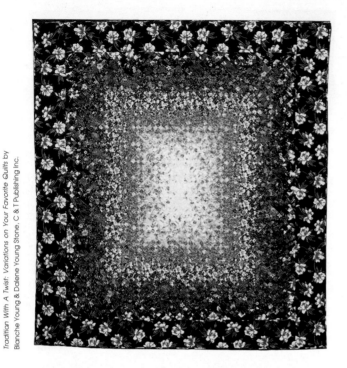

Tradition With A Twist: Variations on Your Favorite Quilts by Blanche Young & Dalene Young Stone, C & T Publishing Inc.

Homage to Mary Brown pattern by Patricia Cox, One of a Kind, Minneapolis, MN

SOUTHERN MAGNOLIAS – BLOOMING NINE PATCH, 91" x 101", PATRICIA C. KILMARK, ATLANTA, GA, QUILTED BY REGINA CARTER.   **819**

820   **HOMAGE TO MARY BROWN,** 100" x 100", ARDETH LAAKE, BELMOND, IA, OPAL ELLINGSTON, AND ADEAN DORR.

MONOGRAM, 68" x 92", HILA LESLIE, NITEROI, RIO DE JANEIRO, BRAZIL, AND VANESSA LOTT.   **821**

822   **AUTUMN GATHERINGS,** 108" x 108", MARQUETTE CO. QUILTERS ASSOCIATION, MARQUETTE, MI, QUILTED BY RONI WEAVER.

Fall Harvest by Ann Seely, Quilter's Newsletter Magazine, Oct. 2000

ANNIVERSARY QUILT, 91" x 91", ETTA McFARLAND, OLIVE BRANCH, MS, QUILTED BY ARLENE ABERNATHY.

THANK YOU CARRIE HALL, 88" x 88", KATHY MUNKELWITZ, ISLE, MN, QUILTED BY BRENDA LEINO. *Second Place*

THE VICTORIAN ERA, 68" x 99", SANDRA MUELLER & FRIENDS, THE WOODLANDS, TX, QUILTED BY LINDA WALSH.

SPARKLE PLENTY, 95" x 95", CLAUDIA CLARK MYERS, DULUTH, MN, AND MARILYN BADGER. *Longarm Machine Quilting award*

823	824
825	826

Carrie Hall Blocks by Bettina Havig, American Quilter's Society

Bernina Machine Workmanship Award

THE SPACE QUILT, 87" x 87", SUE NICKELS, ANN ARBOR, MI, AND PAT HOLLY.

KRAZY KALEIDOSCOPE, 90" x 90", KAY NICKOLS, LAINGSBURG, MI, AND VICKI BREUKER.

| 827 | 828 |
| 829 | 830 |

RHAPSODY IN BLUE, 84" x 84", NORTHWEST SUBURBAN QUILTERS GUILD (NSQG), SYLVAN LAKE, IL, QUILTED BY EVELYN MUELLER.

FLORAL WINDOWS, 86" x 112", PEACE RIVER QUILTERS GUILD, INC., PUNTA GORDA, FL.

The Block Book© 1988, Judy Martin

STARS AND STRIPES AND STREAMERS, 67" x 92", NANCY PETERS & FRIENDS, WILDWOOD, MO, QUILTED BY MARILYN LANGE.

SURPRISE SUNRISE, 103" x 103", BARBARA PTASHINSKI, SURPRISE, AZ, AND JANICE EARLY.

ROSE MEDALLION, 103" x 103", THE PIONEER QUILTERS AND THERESA BOOCK, EUGENE, OR.

PRIDE OF THE PRAIRIE, 88" x 88", SALT CREEK QUILTERS GUILD, WESTERN SPRINGS, IL.

| 831 | 832 |
| 833 | 834 |

Dandelion Wine, McCall's Quilting, January 1994

Illinois Star: 50 Fabulous Paper-Pieced Stars by Carol Doak, Martingale & Co.; Wildflowers: Designs for Appliqué & Quilting and Wild Birds: Designs for Appliqué & Quilting by Carol Armstrong, C & T Publishing Inc.

Cornucopia pattern, *Quiltmaker* magazine;
Carpenter's Wheel Log Cabin pattern, House of White Birches

A PROMISE KEPT (FINALLY), 89" x 89", THERESA SHOSTAK, GREENE, ME, AND LORETTA PELLETIER.

MAUI NO KA OI, 68" x 92", SETSUKO SOFUE & FRIENDS, EBINA, KANAGAWA, JAPAN.

835 836

837 838

OLD FASHIONED FAMILY ROSE, 90" x 108", VICKI SPIERING & FAMILY, WAUWATOSA, WI.

A LIFE SHARED TOGETHER, 97" x 94", CARLA STEHR, SEATTLE, WA, AND WANDA RAINS.

Designs used and exhibited with permission of The Walt Disney Company

Honorable Mention

NEW BEGINNINGS/EXPANDING FRIENDSHIPS, 88" x 110", MARCIA STEVENS & FRIENDS, BRAINERD, MN.

FABRIC FRENZY, 88" x 104", PEG SWARTZ, HARRISBURG, MO, AND BOON-SLICK TRAIL QUILTERS' GUILD, QUILTED BY MO. UNITED METH. WOMEN.

839 840
841 842

WHERE'S BOO?, 65" x 85", JAN STEWART, SAN DIEGO, CA, AND PHYLLIS STRICKLAND.

GOLDEN ANNIVERSARY, 94" x 106", THURSDAY QUILTING FRIENDS, MADISON, WI.

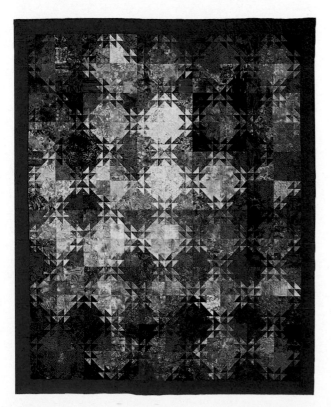

Watercolor Basket by Patchworks Country Pattern Company; Winter Rose by Barbara Brande-burg, Cabbage Rose; Perennial Patchwork by Jackie Robinson, Animas Quilts Publishing

Garden Stepping Stones, Leslie Beck, Fiber Mosaics

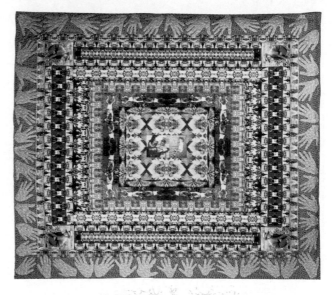

DRAGONFLY SUMMER DREAMS, 88" x 108", SALLIE TOWNSEND-HUGHES, STUART, FL, BARBARA LOGULLO.

843 **844**

845 **846**

FRIENDSHIP GARDEN, 82" x 82", WEST MICHIGAN QUILTERS GUILD, GRAND RAPIDS, MI.

WEDDING QUILT FOR CHRIS & JULIA, 82" x 92", BARBARA WEBSTER, BURNSVILLE, NC, AND HEATHER ROGERS.

ORCHID WREATH, 84" x 84", PAM CRAIG, CHRIS HALL, CLEO HAMILTON, KATHY WILSON, ST. CHARLES, MO.

Forget-Me-Knots by Jeana Kimball, Foxglove Studio

The Romance of the Patchwork Quilt, Carrie A. Hall & Rose G. Kretsinger, Dover Publications

"Floral Medallion" chapter, *Wisconsin Quilts: Stories in the Stitches*, Howell Press

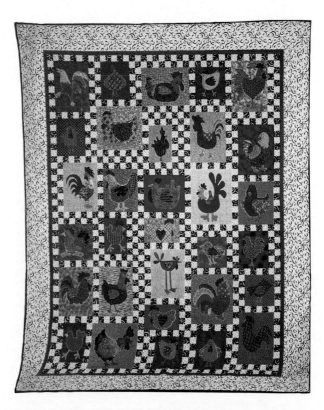

Frog Pond by Shar Jorgenson, *Quilting from the Heartland*; Freddy's House: *Brilliant Color in Quilts*, Freddy Moran, C & T Publishing Inc.

First Place

JO'S GARDEN, 73" x 83", WISCONSIN QUILTERS INC. 2003 RAFFLE QUILT COM., JOANN JACOBI, AND PENNY GERDS. EAST TROY, WI.

847 **848**
901 **902**

BECAUSE IT'S THERE! 80" x 94", BETTY ALVAREZ, MARIETTA, GA.

GLOBAL VILLAGE, 93" x 86", WOMEN WITHOUT BORDERS, HARRISON TOWNSHIP, MI.

HOT & SPICY WINGS, 71" x 88", DOROTHY L. BONOMO, GEORGETOWN, IL.

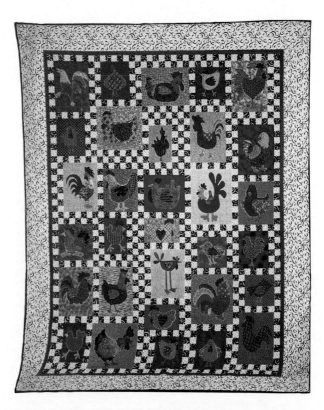

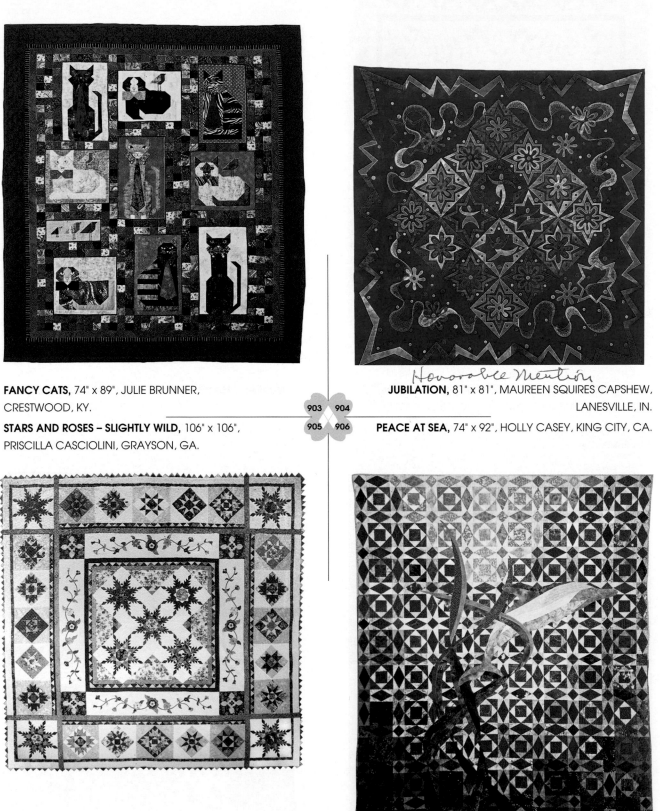

Ties & Tales pattern, judydidit designs

Prickly Pear pattern by Karen K. Stone, Dallas, TX: Workshop with Libby Lehman

Feathered Star by Marsha McCloskey, Quick Classic Quilts. Oxmoor House: My Perfection quilt by Stephanie Broskey on the December 1994 cover of Quilter's Newsletter

Honorable Mention

FANCY CATS, 74" x 89", JULIE BRUNNER, CRESTWOOD, KY.

STARS AND ROSES – SLIGHTLY WILD, 106" x 106", PRISCILLA CASCIOLINI, GRAYSON, GA.

JUBILATION, 81" x 81", MAUREEN SQUIRES CAPSHEW, LANESVILLE, IN.

PEACE AT SEA, 74" x 92", HOLLY CASEY, KING CITY, CA.

903 904
905 906

SNOWFLAKES, 71" x 95", HAEOK CHANG, SEOUL, SOUTH KOREA.

BALTIMORE ALBUM, 98" x 98", MARY ELLEN GLASSMEYER, TUALATIN, OR.

907 | 908
909 | 910

IN-SINUATION, 62" x 86", EVELYN W. DRAKE, McCONNELL, IL.

THE LILY OF THE VALLEY, 89" x 106", TREVA GURLEY, ADA, OK.

Baltimore Beauties & Beyond: Studies in Classic Album Quilt Appliqué by Elly Sienkiewicz, C & T Publishing Inc.

Inspired by stained glass windows, First Baptist Church, Ada, OK.

SNOW MANDALA, 80" x 80", MASAKO HATA, SAGAMIHARA, KANAGAWA, JAPAN.

SORA RANMAN, 72" x 84", SHIGEKO INOUE, KURASHIKI, OKAYAMA, JAPAN.

911 912
913 914

MY FLOWER GARDEN, 90" x 90", KARI HAWKINS, HUNTSVILLE, AL.

SQUARES EVERYWHERE, 108" x 108", MARIE KRISKY, PITTSBURGH, PA.

Pine Tree Quilts by Lois Embree Arnold, American Quilter's Society

LIVE OAK TREE VARIATION, 98" x 98", DONNA LANMAN, DAVENPORT, IA.

PEACE AND HAPPINESS ON EARTH, 91" x 91", EMIKO MURAMATSU, NAKAKOMA, YAMANASHI, JAPAN.

915 916
917 918

LEGACY, 83" x 100", JOAN E. LeBLANC, TERRYTOWN, LA

GARDEN PARTY, 86" x 86", FRANCES MURPHY, BREWSTER, MA.

Little Brown Bird: Masterpiece Appliqué, Margaret Docherty, American Quilter's Society

MAI, 82" x 88", MOMOE NITTA, KAWAGUCHI, SAITAMA, JAPAN.

LOG RING FOR MY DAUGHTER, 80" x 80", FUMIKO OHKAWA, KOBE, HYOGO, JAPAN.

919 920
921 922

BALTIMORE ALBUM (UNICORNS), 96" x 96", HELEN A. O'DWYER, BAYSIDE, NY.

GARDEN SPLENDOR, 87" x 87", MARCIA OLSON, ANKENY, IA.

Unicorn - Glade Interlude pattern by Audle Rye; Workshop with Claire Oehler

Dimensional Appliqué and Baltimore Album Quilts, Elly Sienkiewicz, C & T Publishing Inc.; More Conway Album Blocks: Hearts, Baskets, and Conway Album: I'm Not From Baltimore by Irma Gail Hatcher

Curves in Motion: Quilt Designs & Techniques by Judy B. Dales, C & T Publishing Inc.; Workshop with Gail Garber

Four wreaths from Quick Watercolor Quilts by Dina Pappas, Martingale & Co. Inc.

Shining Star Quilts© 1977, Judy Martin; Encyclopedia of Classic Quilt Patterns, Oxmoor House

LEONID METEOR STORM, 67" x 89", KAREN OWSLEY, MOSCOW, ID.

LONE STAR MEMORIES, 104" x 104", JOYCE SCHAEFER, ARLINGTON HEIGHTS, IL.

923 924
925 926

JOEL'S GARDEN, 82" x 85", JUDY L. ROSS, TRAVERSE CITY, MI.

MADAM KANG'S ROSES, 83" x 83", KANG SEUNGJA, KOBE, JAPAN.

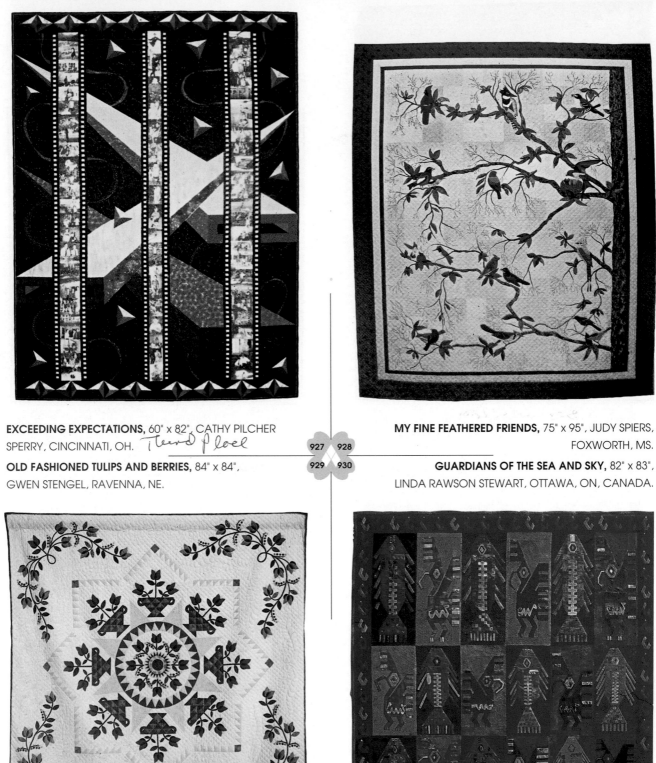

Threadplay workshop with Libby Lehman

Birds in Full View pattern by Alice Wilhoit Designs

Tulip pattern from *Patchwork Quilts, Lady's Circle Editors Choice, 1986*

EXCEEDING EXPECTATIONS, 60" x 82", CATHY PILCHER SPERRY, CINCINNATI, OH.

OLD FASHIONED TULIPS AND BERRIES, 84" x 84", GWEN STENGEL, RAVENNA, NE.

MY FINE FEATHERED FRIENDS, 75" x 95", JUDY SPIERS, FOXWORTH, MS.

GUARDIANS OF THE SEA AND SKY, 82" x 83", LINDA RAWSON STEWART, OTTAWA, ON, CANADA.

927 928
929 930

Shining Star Quilts© 1977, Judy Martin; Encyclopedia of Classic Quilt Patterns, Oxmoor House

Second Place

LONE STAR RISING, 82" x 82", CAROL STREET, VIENNA, IL.

ANTIQUE STARS, 66" x 89", CYNTHIA VICK, WAUWATOSA, WI.

931 932
933 934

BALTIMORE BLUES, 84" x 84", SHOBHA VENUGOPALAN, FRANKLIN, WI.

THE COWBOY QUILT, 60" x 83", CATHY WIGGINS, MACON, NC.

Patterns from Baltimore Album Quilts, Baltimore Beauties & Beyond, Dimensional Appliqué, and Best of Baltimore Beauties by Elly Sienkiewicz, C & T Publishing Inc.; Stop and Smell the Roses border from Borders & Finishing Touches, Bonnie K. Browning, American Quilter's Society

Ancient Stars, Legacies of Love, Susan Garman

Dear Jane®, Brenda Papadakis, used with permission

JANE SINGS THE BLUES, 80" x 80", MARY ELLEN ZEITZ, SOUTH WINDSOR, CT.

STARRING THE LADIES, 18" x 18", CONNIE CHUNN, WEBSTER GROVES, MO.

935	1001
1002	1003

Workshop with Noriko Shimano

MY SWEET DIAMONDS, 17" x 17", YOKO ADACHI, ASHIKAGA, TOCHIGI, JAPAN.

FAÇADE XI, 11" x 14", ROSEMARY CLAUS-GRAY, DONIPHAN, MO.

KAUAI CHICKEN STAR, 18" x 19", SUSAN K. CLEVELAND, WEST CONCORD, MN.

WELCOME TO MY GARDEN, 12" x 12", CATHERINE ERICKSON, WASHOUGAL, WA.

| 1004 | 1005 |
| 1006 | 1007 |

A TOUCH OF MAUVE, 18" x 18", JUDITH DAY, LINDFIELD, NSW, AUSTRALIA.

RASPBERRIES ON THE SIDE, 19" x 19", ANNA FELL, GEORGETOWN, TX.

A VISIT TO PROVENCE, 23" x 24", DIANE GAUDYNSKI, PEWAUKEE, WI.

first place

FEATHERED LOG CABINS, 18" x 18", HELEN JACOBSON, MAXWELL, IA.

1008 1009
1010 1011

Third place

FIFTY BIRDS, 12" x 14", PAT HOLLY, MUSKEGON, MI.

THE BRIGHT FUTURE, 17" x 17", SATOKO KASE, SUMIDA, TOKYO, JAPAN.

Log Cabin: Rediscovered by Machine, Brenda Brayfield, American Quilter's Society

Workshop with Noriko Shimano

Honorable Mention

EPOCH-MAKING, 17" x 17", CHIZUKO KOJIMA, ASHIKAGI, TOCHIGI, JAPAN.

GOLDEN ARRAY, 15" x 17", DIANE LANE, WICHITA, KS.

1012	1013
1014	1015

JAZZ TOO, 17" x 22", PAT KROTH, VERONA, WI.

FLOWER'S BLOOM, 16" x 21", LINDA McLAUGHLIN, RENO, NV.

Workshop with Sally Collins

Coxcomb, Antique Quilts, McCall's Needleworks & Crafts

ANASAZI BASKETS, 12" x 14", DIANE M. MILLER, FALLBROOK, CA.

A MINIATURE ROSE GARDEN FOR JESSIE, 16" x 16", MARTHA A. NORDSTRAND, SAN DIEGO, CA.

Second place

1016 1017
1018 1019

Honorable Mention

WILDWOOD FLOWERS, 22" x 24", MARIE MOORE, HOUSTON, TX.

LA PETIT, 22" x 24", JOANIE ZEIER POOLE, SUN PRAIRIE, WI.

Spray of Roses & Wreath pattern, Martha Orffutt, Bernadine's Needle Art

MAMA'S ROSE GARDEN, 22" x 24", RUTH POTTER,
KERRVILLE, TX.

WATER DANCE, 10" x 12", JANET STEADMAN,
CLINTON, WA.

1020 1021
1022 1023

FALL FOLLIES, 23" x 23", RAINY STEVENS,
LEBANON, ME.

JUNGLE FEVER, 18" x 18", SUE TURNQUIST,
KALAMAZOO, MI.

Dear Pin Pal, Piece O'Cake Designs

LILIES OF THE FIELD, 76" x 76", JANET ATKINS, ATHENS, NY.

FLOATING WITH THE STARS, 42" x 59",
MARGARET BARCLAY, McHENRY, IL.

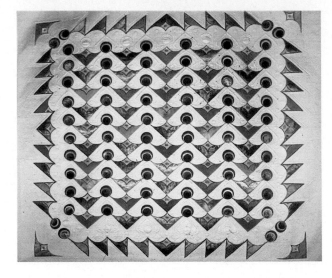

HIBISCUS, 59" x 59", MAGGIE BARBER,
WANDSWORTH COMMON, LONDON, ENGLAND.

BESTIARY, 53" x 72", JULIE BERNUCCI,
SPRINGFIELD, OR.

1101 1102
1103 1104

Vermont Star Party, That Quilt Patch (Fairfax, VA) by Leslie Ann Pfeifer

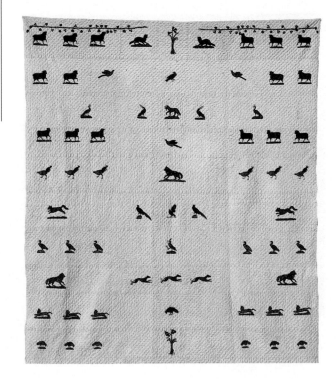

WONDERFUL WORLD OF COLOR, 58" x 74", CATHERINE P. BOYLE, PITTSBURGH, PA..

SOCCER FEVER, 64" x 72", EUN RYOUNG CHOI, SEOUL, KOREA.

1105 1106
1107 1108

ANTONIO'S DREAM, 47" x 57", PAT BUSBY, LAKE OSWEGO, OR.

STARS OF YESTERDAY, 48" x 65", LINDA DYKEN, MOBILE, AL.

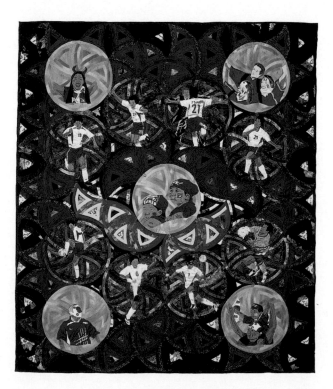

THE SURVIVORS, 41" x 42", ANIKO FEHER, OAK PARK, MI.

GREEN THUMB, 43" x 65", HARRIETT FOX,
NORCROSS, GA.

Second place

BLUE NINE, 42" x 54", MERRY FITZGERALD,
LAKE GROVE, NY.

DOME #3: NATIONAL AIRPORT, 53" x 60",
NANCY GOODMAN, MOBILE, AL.

1109 | 1110
1111 | 1112

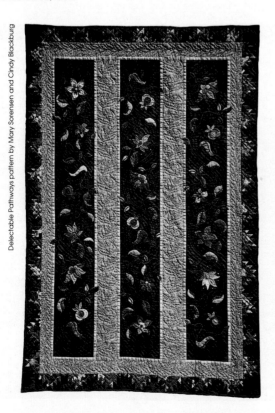

Delectable Pathways pattern by Mary Sorensen and Cindy Blackburg

CHILDHOOD, 53" x 75", VIRGINIA S. GREAVES, OXFORD, AL.

THE WIND CRIES MARY, 52" x 44", JO GROOMS, CHELAN, WA. *First place*

SLIGHTLY ON EDGE, 51" x 51", SHERRIE GROB, MURPHYSBORO, IL.

TWINKLING LOVE FLOWER, 79" x 79", IKUKO HAGINO, YOKOHAMA, KANAGAWA, JAPAN.

1113 1114
1115 1116

Delectable Mountains pattern. *Quilts Galore: Quiltmaking Styles and Techniques,* Diana McClun & Laura Nownes, Quilt Digest Press; *Guide to Machine Quilting,* Diane Gaudynski. American Quilter's Society.

Borders & Finishing Touches, Bonnie K. Browning, American Quilter's Society; Flower patterns by Susan R. DuLaney, Distinctive Pieces; Bee Creative, Ravenwood Designs; Butterflies & Blooms by Carol Armstrong, C & T Publishing Inc.; *Wildflowers* by Carol Armstrong, C & T Publishing Inc.; *The Best of Baltimore Beauties* by Elly Sienkiewicz, C & T Publishing Inc.; *Baltimore Bouquets* by Mimi Dietrich, That Patchwork Place

IN FOCUS, 54" x 54", SUSAN LIIMATTA HORN, SEA CLIFF, NY.

Third Place

BRILLIANT FIREWORKS, 78" x 78", ETSUKO IITAKA, KODAIRA, TOKYO, JAPAN.

HUMMINGBIRD FANTASY, 51" x 55", PAMELA HUMPHRIES, LARKSPUR, CO.

TWEET, 51" x 44", PAT CHESHIRE JENNINGS, BEREA, KY.

Honorable Mention

1117 1118
1119 1120

Magic Stack-n-Whack Quilts®, Bethany S. Reynolds, American Quilter's Society; inspired by Linda V. Taylor quilts.

BUGS IN MY GARDEN, 75" x 59", KAREN JUREK, COCHRANE, AB, CANADA.

MY QUILTS TOWN, 68" x 68", MASAKO KATOH, KASHIMA, IBARAKI, JAPAN.

1121 1122
1123 1124

GRASS WAVE, 77" x 79", MITSUKO KANEDA, HITACHIOTA, IBARAKI, JAPAN.

GROWTH RING, 59" x 63", YUKO KAWAKAMI, KUMAMOTO, JAPAN.

Liberty's Eagle pattern by Barbara Brackman: Baltimore Tribute Pictorial by Mary Sorensen; Baltimore Album Quilts, Baltimore Beauties and Beyond Vols. I & II, Elly Sienkiewicz, C & T Publishing Inc.

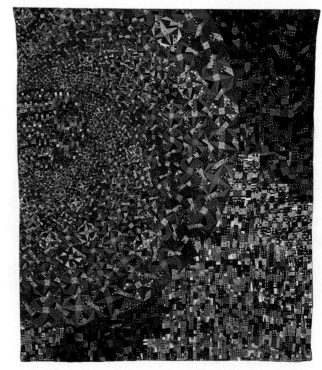

THOSE WERE THE DAYS, 54" x 56", SYLVIA KETONEN,
PT. CHARLOTTE, FL.

CHEERS!, 72" x 66", HIDEKO KUBOTA,
YOKOHAMA, JAPAN.

| 1125 | 1126 |
| 1127 | 1128 |

ETERNITY, 76" x 76", NORIKO KOBAYASHI,
YOKOHAMA, JAPAN.

VORTEX, 67" x 77", TERUMI KURATA,
KUMAGAYA, SAITAMA, JAPAN.

Workshop with Noriko Shinano

Byzantine Garden, a pattern designed by Maggie Walker, Elverson, PA.

ILLUSION, 46" x 46", VANESSA LOTT, RIO DE JANEIRO, BRAZIL.

CHARLOTTE'S WEB, 51" x 51", CHARLOTTE McRANIE, MARIETTA, GA.

1129 1130

1131 1132

OUT OF AFRICA, 55" x 74", NANCY STERETT MARTIN, OWENSBORO, KY.

LONE STAR OF AFRICA, 60" x 60", ALICE MEANS, BOLTON, CT.

Best of Baltimore Beauties, Baltimore Beauties and Beyond, and Best of Baltimore Beauties Vol. II, Elly Sienkiewicz, C & T Publishing Inc.; Rorschach and Lacework patterns, Garden City Gateworks; border inspired by Bethlehem Star by Laura Nownes, Quilts of Thimble Creek, Leisure Arts; workshop with Patricia German

Lone Star Quilts & Beyond by Jan Krentz, C&T Publishing Inc.

Le Fleurs du Jardin, Village Classics Collection, Indygo Junction

THE WARMTH OF PEACE, 78" x 78", YONEKO MIZUNOE, BUNGO TAKADA, OITA, JAPAN.

FROM THE GARDEN TO THE VASE, 56" x 59", RUBY NISHIO, LOS ANGELES, CA.

| 1133 | 1134 |
| 1135 | 1136 |

HOW DOES MY GARDEN GROW? VERY SLOWLY, 62" x 75", PATRICIA MYERS, CARTERSVILLE, GA.

EXOTIC JAPAN, 59" x 65", MICHIKO NODA, FUJISAWA, KANAGAWA, JAPAN.

Roseville, a pattern designed by Maggie Walker, Elverson, PA

PUA PAKE, 42" x 42", BONNIE OUELLETTE, SENECA, SC.

LA PALETTE DE NICOLE, 66" x 61", MARION PERRAULT, BEACONSFIELD, QUEBEC, CANADA.

1137 1138
1139 1140

HELIOS CORONA, 66" x 45", SANDRA PETERSON, MUNCIE, IN.

FIESTA, 53" x 59", JEANNE PFISTER, KAUKAUNA, WI.

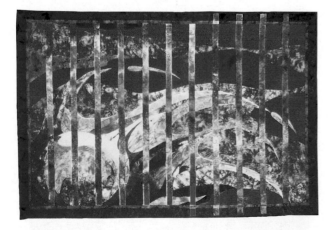

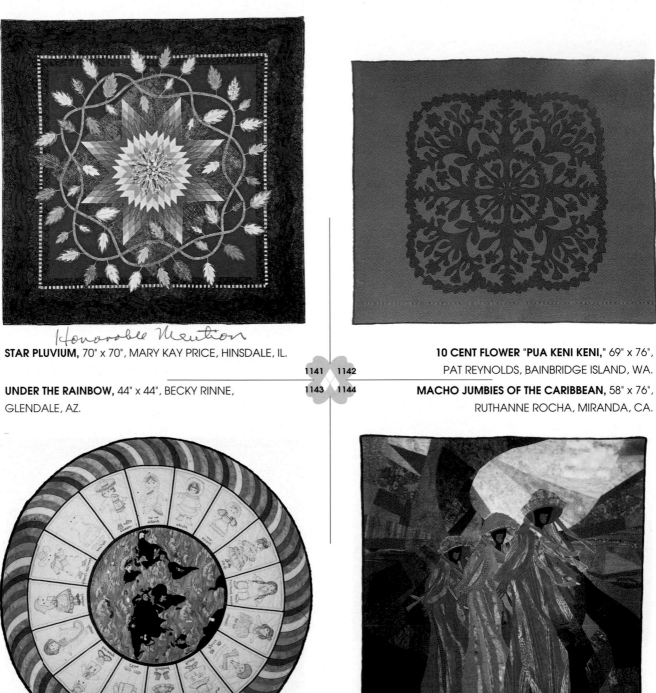

Honorable Mention

STAR PLUVIUM, 70" x 70", MARY KAY PRICE, HINSDALE, IL.

1141 1142

UNDER THE RAINBOW, 44" x 44", BECKY RINNE, GLENDALE, AZ.

1143 1144

Adapted from a Chong Piing pattern

10 CENT FLOWER "PUA KENI KENI," 69" x 76", PAT REYNOLDS, BAINBRIDGE ISLAND, WA.

MACHO JUMBIES OF THE CARIBBEAN, 58" x 76", RUTHANNE ROCHA, MIRANDA, CA.

Aunt Martha's Children of the World I, Colonial Patterns, Inc.

Trapunto designs from *Exploring Machine Trapunto* by Hari Walner,
C & T Publishing Inc.: workshop with Diane Gaudynski

SHAZAM, 66" x 66", LINDA ROSS, LAKE ST. LOUIS, MO.

IN A HEARTBEAT, 50" x 57", MAURINE ROY, EDMONDS, WA.

1145 1146

1147 1148

FOOTSTEPS OF SPRING, 79" x 80", EMIKO SHINODA, NAGOYA, JAPAN.

MARBLED MADNESS #2, 50" x 51", LUCY SILLIMAN, FORT SCOTT, KS.

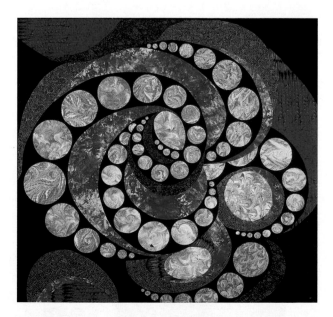

Woven Verdure by Michelle Hill. *Down Under Quilts,* Issue 62, 2002.

BELLFLOWERS, 60" x 75", NANCY SLOAN, FORNEY, TX.

1149 · 1150
1151 · 1152

BLUEBIRD DAYS, 41" x 54", ELIZABETH LEE STEHLIK, LANDRUM, SC.

LEATHER PUPPET, 49" x 76", LINDA RAWSON STEWART, OTTAWA, ON, CANADA.

YO, ADAM! BOOP-OOP-A-DOO!, 76" x 77", GRACE STINTON, MIDLAND, MI.

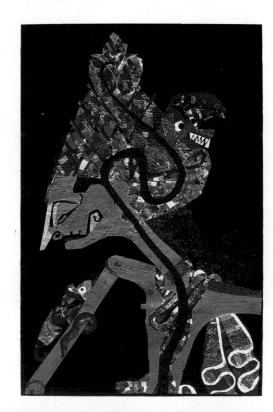

A Country Journal, a pattern designed by Maggie Walker, Elverson, PA

A Quilted for Christmas pattern by Donna Hanson Eines, That Patchwork Place

FANCY FEATHERS, 47" x 53", PATTY STONE, POPLAR BLUFF, MO.

1153 1154

PRINCESS FEATHER, 64" x 64", LORETTA C. SYLVESTER, PALM COAST, FL.

1155 1156

Wall Quiet - Hand Workmanship award

RIPPLE (HAMON), 73" x 73", AKEMI SUGIYAMA, TOKYO, JAPAN.

FLOWERS ARE FRIENDS OF LIFE, 73" x 73", FUSAKO TAKIDO, SHIZUOKA, JAPAN.

Blooms & Baskets by Emily Senuta, American Quilter's Society

Wheels of Whimsy, Better Homes and Gardens American Patchwork & Quilting Quilt Sampler 1999

JOY, 57" x 57", JOAN C. TEMPLE, PITTSBURGH, PA.

MY FAVORITE FLOWER POT, 56" x 65", KYOKO WAKUYA, SUMA, KOBE, JAPAN.

1157   1158
1159   1160

RADIANT CIRCLES, 41" x 41", CYNTHIA VICK, WAUWATOSA, WI.

NORWEGIAN ROSEMALING, 42" x 43", TRUDY SØNDROL WASSON, EDEN PRAIRIE, MN.

Workshop with Kathy Nakajima

TENNESSEE GARLAND, 48" x 48", LINDA WEBSTER, APPLETON, WI.

| 1161 | 1162 |
| 1201 | 1202 |

BIRD IN HAND, 46" x 55", PAMELA ALLEN, KINGSTON, ONTARIO, CANADA.

DAWN OF THE PEACE, 78" x 78", MOTOMURA YUMIKO, ATAKE, TOKUSHIMA, JAPAN.

FOR MATAJI, 52" x 52", ALLISON ALLER, WASHOUGAL, WA.

Workshop with Victoria A. Brown

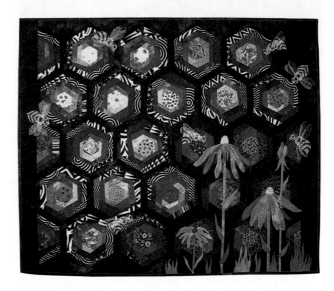

THE WELL, 48" x 78", ESTERITA AUSTIN, PORT JEFFERSON STATION, NY.

RIO GRANDE, 56" x 56", ARLENE L. BLACKBURN, MILLINGTON, TN.

1203 1204
1205 1206

HONEYCOMB, 59" x 50", BARBARA BARR, LITTLETON, CO.

CHOPSTICK CHALLENGE, 74" x 74", PATRICE PERKINS CRESWELL, AUSTIN, TX.

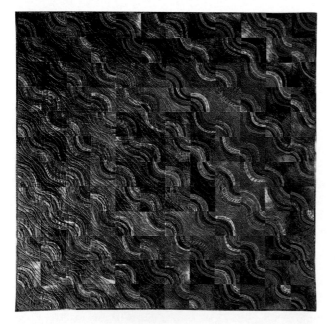

Third Place

TRUMPET LILIES, 40" X 46", DEBRA M. DANKO, GRAND BLANC, MI.

SUNDAY BLOOMERS, 53" x 69", MICKEY DEPRE, OAK LAWN, IL.

| 1207 | 1208 |
| 1209 | 1210 |

AUNTIE GREEN'S GARDEN, 58" x 66", JUDITH DAY, LINDFIELD, NSW, AUSTRALIA.

TRIPLE FEATHER WREATH, 44" x 44", JANET DOVE, McPHERSON, KS.

Amish: The Art of the Quilt by Robert Hughes, Knopf

NATIVE WEAVINGS: SUMMER, 43" x 43", SHERRI BAIN DRIVER, CENTENNIAL, CO.

MIDNIGHT MADNESS, 48" x 48", BARBARA L. ELKINS, YUKON, OK.

| 1211 | 1212 |
| 1213 | 1214 |

GEARS TO YOU!, 41" x 43", ROBBI JOY EKLOW, THIRD LAKE, IL.

NOT AVAILABLE

Lone Star Quilts & Beyond by Jan Krentz, C & T Publishing Inc.

TRIANGLES AND BEADS II, 67" x 67", ANN FAHL, RACINE, WI.

Wall Quilt — Machine Workmanship Award

MIDNIGHT FANTASY #6, 48" x 59", CARYL BRYER FALLERT, OSWEGO, IL.

1215 1216

1217 1218

THESE COLORS DON'T RUN, 50" x 50", SHIRLEY FLETCHER, ORANGE, CA.

HANGING BASKET, 68" x 77", KAZUKO FUNABASAMA, OHTA, JAPAN.

Flags & Eagles, *Quilter's Newsletter* July 1985, cover photo by Clay H. Kappelman

BLACK HOLE, 53" x 48", GAIL GARBER, ALBUQUERQUE, NM.

1219   1220

COME FLY WITH ME, 47" x 65", ANNELIES GHYSELEN, HITACHINAKA, NAZARETH, BELGIUM.

DEEP WOODS REFLECTION, 42" x 42", PATRICIA GOULD, ANGEL FIRE, NM.

1221   1222

CAROLINA SUNSHINE, 60" x 60", SARADEAN HALLMAN, WEST COLUMBIA, SC.

Inspired by a Frederick Church (1826-1900) sketch

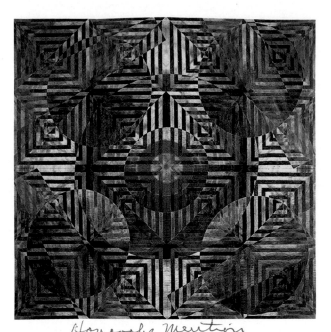

Honorable Mention

SQUARED ILLUSIONS IV, 47" x 47", GLORIA HANSEN, HIGHTSTOWN, NJ.

STONES IN MY GARDEN, 42" x 40", ANGELA J. HAWORTH, SUPERIOR, WI.

MELODIOUS, 65" x 73", SACHIKO HASEGAWA, HITACHINAKA, IBARAKI, JAPAN.

ROSY-ETTA STONES, 40" x 57", DIANNE S. HIRE, NORTHPORT, ME.

1223	1224
1225	1226

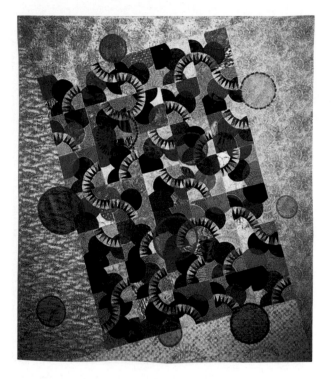

EMILEE'S BUBBLE, 59" x 68", RENE JENNINGS, GROVER BEACH, CA.

TUB TRAFFIC, 59" x 59", REBECCA A. KELLEY WOOD, SIGNAL MOUNTAIN, TN.

1227 | 1228
1229 | 1230

QUEEN OF THE GARDEN, 47" x 59", SUZANNE KISTLER, VISALIA, CA.

RAP-SO-DEE, 45" x 57", PAT KROTH, VERONA, WI.

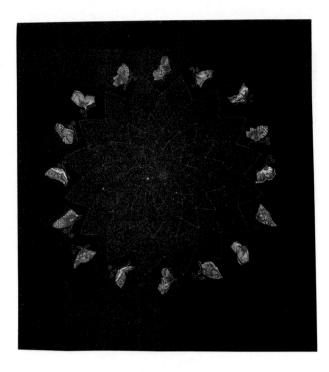

MIDNIGHT DANCE OF THE BUTTERFLY, 63" x 63",
RICHARD LARSON, CARROLLTON, TX.

SPICEY BROWN SUGAR, 41" x 41", LIBBY LOWE,
ALPHARETTA, GA. *Honorable Mention*

1231	1232
1233	1234

KIMONO FLOWERS, 43" x 45", DOROTHY LeBOEUF,
ROGERS, AR.

APRIL SNOW, 56" x 64", JANICE MADDOX,
ASHEVILLE, NC.

7 ROSES – BLACK 'N' WHITE BALL, 41" x 41",
ALBERT MAGGITTI, SANTA FE, NM.

NUMBER NINE DREAM, 61" x 62", NATALIA MANLEY,
LONDON, UNITED KINGDOM.

1235	1236
1237	1238

ABUNDANCE OF ORCHIDS, 49" x 42",
BARBARA BARRICK McKIE, LYME, CT.

SPARKS, 46" x 46", SUSAN NELSON, PRIOR LAKE, MN.

Block Factory Co., Mariner's Compass Edition: workshop with Gwen Lundgren

PRISMATIC FLOWERS, 71" x 71", BARBARA OLSON, BILLINGS, MT.

REJOICE IN THE DANCE, 70" x 58", MABETH H. OXENREIDER, CARLISLE, IA.

1239	1240
1241	1242

THE POND, 68" x 47", MARTI PLAGER, LOUISVILLE, KY.

HEIRLOOM ROSES, 55" x 57", SANDRA REED, AURORA, ONT. CANADA.

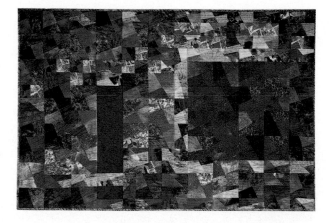

Workshop with Karen McTavish

Inspired by Franz Marc (1880-1916) paintings and puzzle quilt by Robbi Joy Eklow. Third Lake, IL.

CONCATENATION, 45" x 60", JERI RIGGS, DOBBS FERRY, NY.

1243 1244

1245 1246

STARLIGHT MOSAIC, 51" x 52", SHARON V. ROTZ, MOSINEE, WI.

OPPOSITES ATTRACT, 46" x 51", PAULINE SALZMAN, TREASURE ISLAND, FL.

GALENA GLORY, 57" x 57", CYNTHIA POLLARD SCHMITZ, ARLINGTON HTS., IL.

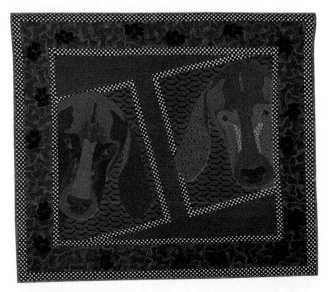

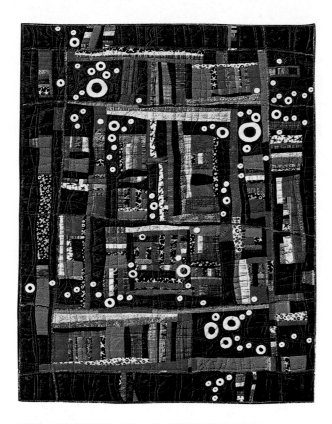

NEED A LIFESAVER?, 46" x 60", KAREN HULL SIENK, COLDEN, NY.

NO TIME TO WASTE, 75" x 56", CAROL ANN SINNREICH, LAWTON, OK.

1247	1248
1249	1250

A FINE ROMANCE, 40" x 59", JANET STEADMAN, CLINTON, WA. *First place*

SHADOWED POPPIES, 52" x 52", BONNIE STETSON, PINEHURST, NC.

Italian Tiles pattern by Susan R. Dulaney, Distinctive Pieces; workshop with Linda Fiedler

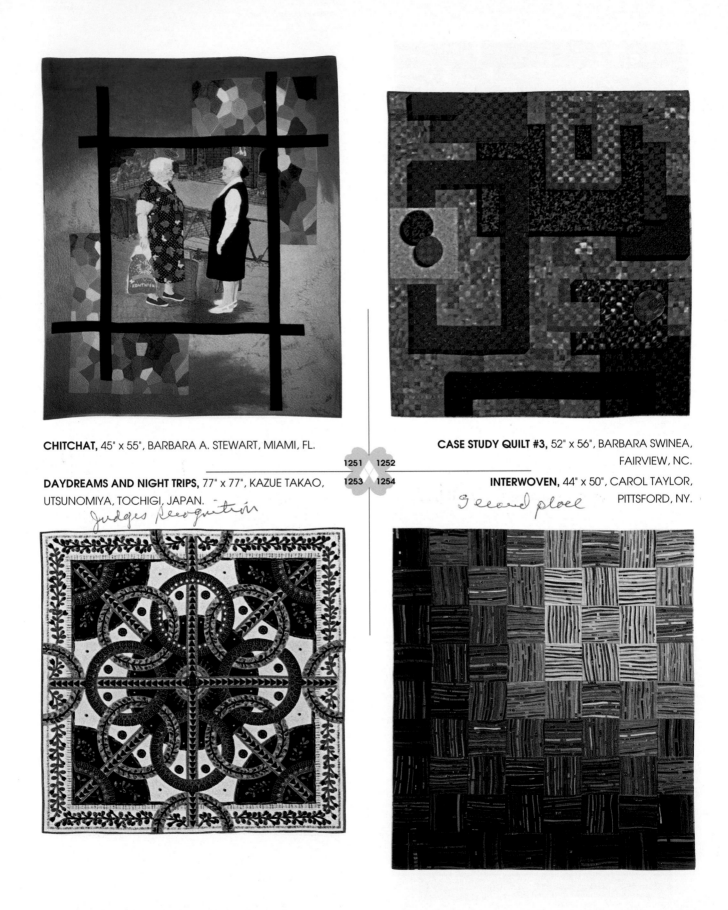

CHITCHAT, 45" x 55", BARBARA A. STEWART, MIAMI, FL.

CASE STUDY QUILT #3, 52" x 56", BARBARA SWINEA, FAIRVIEW, NC.

DAYDREAMS AND NIGHT TRIPS, 77" x 77", KAZUE TAKAO, UTSUNOMIYA, TOCHIGI, JAPAN.

Judges Recognition

INTERWOVEN, 44" x 50", CAROL TAYLOR, PITTSFORD, NY.

Second place

| 1251 | 1252 |
| 1253 | 1254 |

AZTEC SUNRISE, 58" x 58", CINDY VOUGH,
NICHOLASVILLE, KY.

1255 1256

UNEXPECTED PATTERN, 64" x 64", MIEKO WASHIO,
YAO, OSAKA, JAPAN. *Judges Recognition*

1257 1258

STAR LIGHT – STAR BRIGHT, 61" x 61", M. GAYLE WALLACE,
TAYLOR, LA.

CELEBRATION, 42" x 42", RACHEL A. WETZLER,
ST. CHARLES, IL.

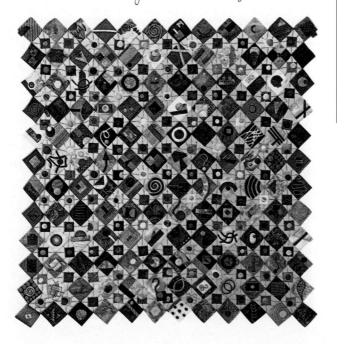

Floral Quatrefoil 1988 by Richard Diens, Goodwood Art Glass Studio, Palantine, IL

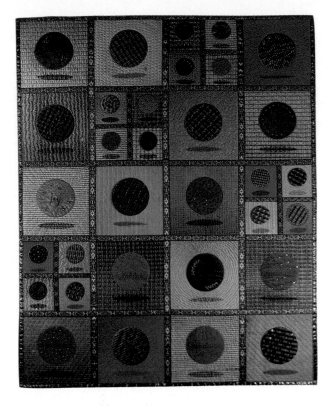

GROOVY BASKET OF BLESSINGS, 40" x 41", AMY STEWART WINSOR, CARY, NC.

TRIPLE TREAT, 40" x 51", JUANITA G. YEAGER, LOUISVILLE, KY.

FRUITS OF THE SPIRIT, 48" x 63", COLLEEN WISE, PUYALLUP, WA.

OZARK PICNIC, 64" x 64", MARLA YEAGER, LITTLETON, CO.

| 1259 | 1260 |
| 1261 | 1262 |

Starlight Garden by Whimsicals, Terri Degenkolb and Jackie Conaway

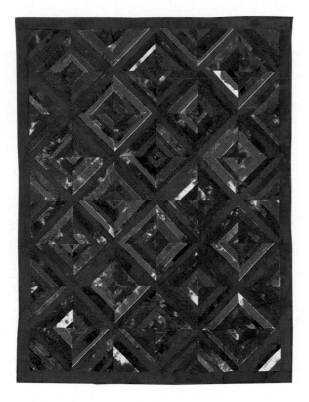

RAINBOW STRINGS, 50" x 66", MADGE ZIEGLER, NEWARK, DE.

JUNE JUBILEE, 70" x 60", FRIEDA ANDERSON, ELGIN, IL.

1263 1301
1302 1303

FISHERMAN JIM, 50" x 68", ROSALIE BAKER, DAVENPORT, IA.

LAGOON OF SCARLET PLUMAGE, 45" x 47", EMILIE M. BELAK, GRAND FORKS, BC, CANADA.

Fisherman Jim

TOGETHER – WE CAN, 43" x 57", WENDY BUTLER BERNS, LAKE MILLS, WI.

QUILT ANGEL, 43" x 77", MARY S. BUVIA, GREENWOOD, IN.

1304 1305
1306 1307

Third place

OH MY, 46" x 50", NANCY S. BROWN, OAKLAND, CA.

BRISTLECONE & BIGHORN, 64" x 54", MONECA CALVERT, RENO, NV.

Honorable Mention

PUSSY CAT, PUSSY CAT, WHERE HAVE YOU BEEN?, 60" x 71", LORRAINE CARTHEW, BRISBANE, QUEENSLAND, AUSTRALIA.

UNBROKEN OAK, 69" x 55", BARBARA LYDECKER CRANE, LEXINGTON, MA.

1308   1309

1310   1311

A BUDDHIST DANCE, 70" x 77", EUN RYOUNG CHOI, SEOUL, KOREA.

GREAT BLUE HERON, 48" x 54", KAREN DONOBEDIAN, BEND, OR

Workshop with Ruth McDowell

MARRIE'S POPPY, 44" x 49", NICOLE M. DUNN, LOS ALAMOS, NM.

AUGUST GARDEN, 49" x 48", ANN FAHL, RACINE, WI.

First Place

THE DAY THE FOG FROZE, 40" x 47", LINDA M. FIEDLER, MEADOWS OF DAN, VA.

1312 | 1313
1314 | 1315

FIRST SIGN OF SPRING, 48" x 60", LAURA FOGG, UKIAH, CA.

SWAN AND LILIES, 58" x 42", KARIN FRANZEN, FAIRBANKS, AK.

SPRING'S CALL, 52" x 45", CATHY GEIER, WAUKESHA, WI.

1316 1317
1318 1319

AEQVANS IONIOS, 78" x 55", CAROL GODDU, MISSISAUGA, ONTARIO, CANADA.

HIGHLAND FAREWELL, 47" x 41", SONIA GRASVIK, SEATTLE, WA.

DALMATIAN DOWNS, 41" x 61", VIRGINIA S. GREAVES, OXFORD, AL.

CELTIC CREED, 53" x 62", DENISE HAVLAN, PALOS HILLS, IL.

1320 1321
1322 1323

CHURCH IN THE WILDWOOD, 65" x 71", ANN J. HARWELL, WENDELL, NC.

HARMONY, 40" x 54", KATHY HEFNER, PEACHTREE CITY, GA.

Internet class with Susan Brittingham

Illustrations by A. Raymond Katz from *Joey the Littlest Clown,* used with permission

CLOWNING AROUND, 62" x 60", ELEANOR L. HICKMAN, ANDERSON, IN.

4TH OF JULY PARADE, 64" x 64", JANINE HOLZMAN, SITKA, AK.

1324 | 1325

1326 | 1327

HILLSDALE COUNTY, 74" x 76", SUE HOLDAWAY-HEYS, ANN ARBOR, MI.

UP FOR SCRATCH, 45" x 51", CYNTHIA JOHNSTONE, GREENVILLE, GA.

Inspired by Erté costume designs

MOON DANCE – HAUTE COUTURE SERIES, 46" x 69", JANE KENNEDY, LONE JACK, MO.

LITTLE GIRL, 48" x 48", MARCIA L. KNOPP, BAY CITY, MI.

1328 1329
1330 1331

LIKE MOTHER, LIKE DAUGHTER, 74" x 49", GLORIA KORN, YARDLEY, PA.

SHELF LIFE, 40" x 72", MARION MACKEY, WEST CHESTER, PA.

Collectibles Quilt II by Wendy Gtzel

UNEASY NEIGHBORS, 47" x 41", SHARON MALEC, WEST CHICAGO, IL.

SUN-BATHING BLUE TIT, 66" x 80", INGE MARDAL, CHANTILLY, FRANCE.

| 1332 | 1333 |
| 1334 | 1335 |

CONTEMPLATION IV, 50" x 66", BONNIE LYN McCAFFERY, HAWLEY, PA.

LILIES IN THE RAIN, 42" x 47", BARBARA BARRICK McKIE, LYME, CT.

Inspired by Adrian Dent painting

TRINITY, 52" x 60", MARTI PLAGER, LOUISVILLE, KY.

1336 1337
1338 1339

GONE AWAY?, 45" x 67", ANNE RAY, LAMBOURN, BERKSHIRE, UNITED KINGDOM.

YARD TOOLS, 45" x 54", PAULINE SALZMAN, TREASURE ISLAND, FL.

YESTERDAY'S TADPOLE, 52" x 52", LOUISE SCHOTZ, IRMA, WI.

Country Journal, cover of May/June 2000 issue, used with permission

YOUNG WINTER, 47" x 59", SUE SOETENGA, EAGLE RIVER, WI.

1340 1341

AMERICA, MY HOME, 58" x 65", PATRICIA L. STYRING, JACKSONVILLE, FL.

OUTFOXED, 49" x 45", LISELOTTE TAN, LA JOLLA, CA.

1342 1343

TROPICAL SIMPLICITY, 42" x 50", B.J. TITUS, COATESVILLE, PA.

Second Place

WARNING: HOUSEWORK MAY BE HAZARDOUS TO YOUR HEALTH, 50" x 64", SUE TURNQUIST, KALAMAZOO, MI.

BRANCHING OUT, 63" x 47", RACHEL WETZLER, ST. CHARLES, IL.

1344 1345
1346 1347

TEA PARTY TIME, 43" x 48", LAURA WASILOWSKI, ELGIN, IL.

THE MAP MAKERS, 56" x 65", CASSANDRA WILLIAMS, GRANTS PASS, OR.

VOGUE MILLINERY, 54" x 55", MARY ABBOTT WILLIAMS, PINEHURST, NC.

WOODLAND TREASURE, 50" x 59", MARLENE BROWN WOODFIELD, LAPORTE, IN.

1348   1349

1401   1402

TURN TURN TURN, 63" x 76", SHIRLEY WOODWORTH ABEL, STOUGHTON, WI, DONNA WOODWORTH WILLADSEN.

A GARDEN FULL OF PLEASURE, 53" x 63", KATHLEEN CAVANESS & FRIENDS, FENTON, MO.

The Manor House Sampler, Elizabeth Quilts, Gaithersburg, MD

Kahla Ennis design, *McCall's Quilting,* June 1999

Honorable Mention

BLIZZARD 12: SHADED ENCHANTMENT, 50" x 50", DANA LACY CHAPMAN, PhD, PLANO, TX, AND TRISTAN ROBIN BLAKEMAN.

BERKELEY SPRINGS DIVERSITY, 47" x 59", ANN C. DARLING, BERKELEY SPRINGS, WV, QUILTED BY JANE FRENKE.

1403 1404
1405 1406

CELEBRATION, 55" x 55", FRANCES E. COLLINS, CHESTERFIELD, MO, AND MEMBERS OF THE BIT x BIT FRIENDSHIP CIRCLE.

ONE MORE BIRD, 59" x 59", PHYLLIS BEAN ENOS, TULSA, OK, QUILTED BY KIM HULL.

There Goes the Neighborhood, *Quilt-Lovers' Favorites, Vol. 2, Better Homes and Gardens*

Block Appliqué patterns by Susan R. DuLaney, Distinctive Pieces

STARLIT GARDEN, 68" x 68", KAREN ESTERHOLDT, QUILTED BY PAT ROCHE, PORTLAND, OR.

1407 1408

1409 1410

THE PAINTERS' GALLERY©, 74" x 73", JEAN M. EVANS, JOYCE MURRIN, MEDINA, OH.

PRAIRIE SALSA, 75" x 75", TRESA JONES, KELLY ASHTON, SENECA, KS.

CRAZY FOR RED, 60" x 72", KATHY KURYLA, KAY ROBERTS, FRANKLIN, TN.

Heartland Album by Kathy Delaney, Kansas City Star

Blocks By The Square by Jodi Barrows, Quiltingly Yours

Ribbon appliqué workshop with Wendy Grande

THE BIRDS & FLOWERS OF HAPPINESS, 69" x 56", LOLITA LUKACH, QUILTED BY JAN WALSH, MILWAUKEE, WI.

FARMLANDS, OUR COUNTRY'S HERITAGE, 64" x 64", NAOMI MacNUTT, FT. MILL, SC, QUILTED BY DEBBIE LEE.

| 1411 | 1412 |
| 1413 | 1414 |

LIGHTHOUSES, 40" x 40", JUDY LUNDBERG, ROSE REMUND, SILVER SPRING, MD.

GULLS IN THE HEAT HAZE, 77" x 51", INGE MARDAL, STEEN HOUGS, CHANTILLY, FRANCE.

First Place

Piecemakers Times and Seasons Quilt Calendar 2003

Tic-Tac-Mo, Atkinson Designs, Inc.

Eucalyptus Wreath, *Botanical Wreaths*, C & T Publishing Inc.

SON, YOU MARRIED A YANKEE, 55" x 75", SARAH NORMAN, AUBURN, AL, QUILTED BY ELIZABETH WALLER.

STAR OF CALIFORNIA, 70" x 70", PAN (POLLY BRECKENRIDGE, ALICE FRIESEN, NANCY PARMELEE), SONOMA, CA.

1415   1416

1417   1418

WANT 2 NECK?, 40" x 50", SHELLI RICCI, APPLE VALLEY, MN, QUILTED BY KIM BRUNNER.

WONKY HOUSES, 52" x 48", DEB RICHARDSON & FRIENDS, EWING, KY.

Floral Abundance: Appliqué Designs Inspired by William Morris. Martingale & Co. Inc.

WE SEEK AFTER THESE THINGS, 60" x 60", ANN SEELY, JOYCE STEWART, TAYLORSVILLE, UT.

1419 1420

TEQUILA SUNSET, 48" x 48", PADDY SHOPHER, CINDY YOUNG, CONCORD, CA. *Second Place*

1421 1422

EVENING AT THE POND, 57" x 45", NATALIE SEWELL, NANCY ZIEMAN, MADISON, WI.

NINTH HOUR, 49" x 55", LYNDON SEW-N-SEWS, TAKOMA PARK, MD.

Workshop with Sally Collins

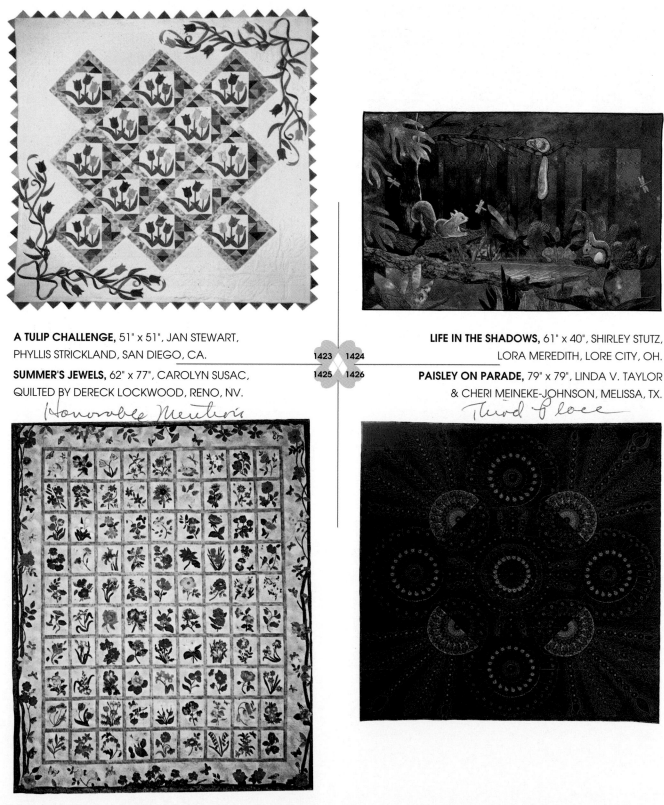

Garden Gate, Picking up the Pieces, Piecemakers

Inspired by *Thread Magic* by Ellen Anne Eddy, Martingale & Co. Inc. and Gwen Fassinger's canvas art

A TULIP CHALLENGE, 51" x 51", JAN STEWART, PHYLLIS STRICKLAND, SAN DIEGO, CA.

SUMMER'S JEWELS, 62" x 77", CAROLYN SUSAC, QUILTED BY DERECK LOCKWOOD, RENO, NV.

LIFE IN THE SHADOWS, 61" x 40", SHIRLEY STUTZ, LORA MEREDITH, LORE CITY, OH.

PAISLEY ON PARADE, 79" x 79", LINDA V. TAYLOR & CHERI MEINEKE-JOHNSON, MELISSA, TX.

1423 1424
1425 1426

Honorable Mention

Third Place

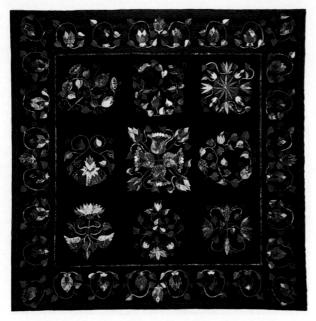

Water Lilies pattern by Ale Rossman, Lotusland's

BLOOMIN FRIENDS, 62" x 62", THURSDAY QUILTERS, GROVER BEACH, CA.

1427

AMERICAN QUILTER'S SOCIETY

2005 QUILT SHOW & Contest

PADUCAH, KENTUCKY

announcing

NEW CONTEST RULES

April 20, 21, 22 & 23, 2005

Paducah Expo Center
Paducah, Kentucky

$100,000+ TOTAL CASH AWARDS

Juried & Judged Show • 400 Quilts Exhibited • Sixteen Categories

$20,000*	Hancock's of Paducah Best of Show
$12,000*	AQS Hand Workmanship Award
$12,000*	Bernina Machine Workmanship Award
$3,000	Gammill Longarm Machine Quilting Award
$5,000*	RJR Best Wall Award
$3,000	McCall's Quilting Wall Hand Workmanship Award
$3,000	Brother Wall Machine Workmanship Award

*Purchase awards – These quilts become the property of the Museum of the American Quilter's Society.

Categories 1– 14	1st Place	$1,500.00
Categories 1– 14	2nd Place	$1,000.00
Categories 1– 14	3rd Place	$750.00
Category 15	1st Place	$400.00
	2nd Place	$300.00
	3rd Place	$200.00

TIMETABLE

January 3, 2005:
Quilt images (slides or digitals on CD-Rom), completed entry blank, and entry fee must be received by AQS, or postmarked, no later than January 3, 2005. Slides of quilts accepted for competition will not be returned. CD's will not be returned for any entries.

March 4, 2005:
All entrants will be notified. If your quilt is accepted, instructions will be included on sending your quilt for judging.

April 8, 2005:
Accepted quilts must be received by the American Quilter's Society, 5801 Kentucky Dam Rd., Paducah, KY 42003.

April 19, 2005:
Awards will be presented at the Awards Presentation (Tuesday evening, April 19), or mailed after the show to those unable to attend.

Quilt Contest Rules

1. Any quiltmaker can enter a **completed** quilt by submitting entry blank, entry fee, and images of the completed work.
2. Limit two entries per person, one quilt per category.
3. Quilt must be constructed and quilted by person(s) named on entry blank.
4. Quilts stitched by one or two persons can be entered in all categories except 5 and 14. Quilts stitched by three or more people can only be entered in Group Categories 5 or 14.
5. All quilts must be quilted by hand, by machine, or both.
6. Quilt must have been finished after 2002 and be in excellent condition.
7. Quilts displayed in any previous AQS contest or made from pre-cut or stamped kits are ineligible.
8. Quilts must be a single unit and not framed with wood, metal, etc.
9. Quilts that combine two or more techniques (other than quilting) should be entered in the Mixed Techniques category (i.e., piecing/appliqué, appliqué/embroidery, piecing/tra-punto, etc.)
10. Quilts in categories 4 and 13 must be a first-time entry in any AQS contest.
11. Quilt Sizes: (Quilts longer than 90" must have the rod pocket sewn 90" from the floor for hanging. A quilt label identifying the maker must be stitched to the back lower edge of the quilt.)
    a. Bed-sized quilts in categories 1 – 5 must be 60" to 110" in width and a minimum length of 80".
    b. Handmade quilts in category 6 must be 60" to 110" in width and 80" or more in length.
    c. Large wall quilts, categories 7 – 9, must be 60" to 110" in width and 60" or more in length.
    d. Small wall quilts, categories 10 – 14, must be 40" to 60" in width and 40" to 60" in length.

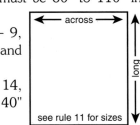
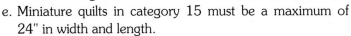

    e. Miniature quilts in category 15 must be a maximum of 24" in width and length.
    f. Youth quilts in category 16 can be any size.
12. Quilt entries in categories 1 – 9 will be considered for the Hancock's of Paducah Best of Show, AQS Hand Workman-ship, and Bernina Machine Workmanship Awards; quilts in categories 10 – 15 are eligible for the RJR Best Small Wall Quilt purchase awards. These four prize-winning quilts will become part of the permanent collection of the Museum of the American Quilter's Society.
13. Quilt must be available for judging and display from April 8 through April 29, 2005.
14. Incomplete, torn, or soiled quilts will not qualify for entry or exhibition.
15. Full-view slide or digital photo must show all edges of the fin-ished quilt. Detail slide or digital photo must show the quilt-ing stitches. Please do not send glass slides.
16. All decisions of the jurors and judges are final. AQS reserves the right to reject any entry, including those that fail to fol-low the quilt contest rules.

17. Please include the complete name and address of your loca newspaper so a news release can be sent there.
18. See Categories for descriptions of each category.

TO ENTER, SEND:

(a) Completed and signed entry blank with correct category circled.
(b) Two 35 mm slides (one full view of **completed** quilt an one detail of **completed** quilt) OR send two digital image with no modification including cropping and color correctio (one full view of **completed** quilt and one detail of **com pleted** quilt) on a CD-Rom, using a minimum of 4 M (megapixel) camera, on highest resolution setting, saved as jpeg or tiff file (be sure to finish the CD and label the dis with your name and title(s) of the work). Photos cannot be mailed and CD's will not be returned. Identifying name(s must not be visible on the quilt in the images.
(c) Entry fee:
AQS members $5.00 per quilt.
Non-members $25.00 per quilt.

CATEGORIES

Bed Quilts – width 60" to 110"; minimum length 80".
  1. Appliqué – predominant technique is appliqué
  2. Pieced – predominant technique is piecing
  3. Mixed Techniques – two or more predominant tech-niques, not including quilting
  4. 1st Entry in an AQS Quilt Contest – any technique
  5. Group – any technique; made by three or more people

Handmade Quilts – width 60" to 110", length 80" or more
  6. Hand – any technique; the entire quilt top must be stitched by hand; backing and binding may be stitched by machine

Large Wall Quilts – width 60" to 110"; length 60" or more
  7. Appliqué – predominant technique is appliqué
  8. Pieced – predominant technique is piecing
  9. Mixed Techniques – two or more predominant tech-niques, not including quilting

Small Wall Quilts – width 40" to 60", length 40" to 60"
  10. Traditional – uses traditional quiltmaking patterns or designs, including variations
  11. Non-traditional – a new creation, not a copy of a previ-ous work
  12. Pictorial – representation of a person, place, or thing
  13. 1st Entry in an AQS Quilt Contest – any technique
  14. Group – any technique, made by three or more people

Miniature Quilts – width 24" maximum, length 24" maximum
  15. Miniature – all aspects of the quilt are in reduced scale

Youth Quilts – any size, for exhibit only (not judged)
  16. Quilts **made by children,** grades K – 12, using any quiltmaking technique(s)

2005 AQS Quilt Contest

Entry Blank to Accompany Slides or CD-Rom (this form may be photocopied)

❐ Member $5.00   ❐ Non-member $25.00

Membership # _____

Entrant's or Group Name _____
                    (Please print)   (This name will be used in the Show Book.)

Street_____ City _____

State _____ Zip_____ Country _____ Postal Code _____

E-mail _____ Phone ( ) _____ Fax ( ) _____

Complete Name of Newspaper _____ Newspaper E-mail _____

Newspaper Mailing Address _____

Circle One Category Number:
(See rule 11 for size)

Bed Quilts:
1. Appliqué
2. Pieced
3. Mixed Techniques
4. 1st Entry in AQS Quilt Contest
5. Group – Bed-sized

Handmade Quilts
6. Hand

Large Wall Quilts
7. Appliqué
8. Pieced
9. Mixed Techniques

Small Wall Quilts
10. Traditional
11. Non-traditional
12. Pictorial
13. 1st Entry in an AQS Quilt Contest
14. Group – Small Wall
15. Miniature
16. Youth

See Categories in the rules for descriptions of each category.

Please put your name on the slide mounts or CD-Rom and mail slides or digital images (as outlined in the rules), completed entry blank, and fee for each quilt to:

American Quilter's Society,
Dept. Paducah Entry,
PO Box 3290, Paducah, KY 42002-3290

Information about your quilt:

Title _____

Size in inches _____ " across x _____ " long; Approx. Insurance Value $ _____
                                        (Over $1,000 requires a written appraisal, maximum value $5,000)

Names(s) of everyone who stitched on this quilt:

_____

_____

Brief Description of Quilt for Show Booklet (25 words)

_____

_____

Techniques: (Choose all that apply)

❐ Appliqué   ❐ Piecing   ❐ Embroidery   ❐ Trapunto   ❐ Other _____

Quilting: (Choose all that apply)   ❐ Hand   or   ❐ Machine

❐ Domestic (Home) Machine   ❐ Machine Quilting Frame System   ❐ Stitch Regulator

❐ Shortarm Quilting Machine   ❐ Longarm Quilting Machine   ❐ Longarm – Hand Guided

Design/Pattern Source (Choose all that apply; Use separate paper for additional space)

❐ Totally Original *(Definition: first; not a copy of a previous work; new creation; patterns by others are not used)*

❐ Pattern(s) used; *list pattern source below*

Magazine	Issue	Year	Project Title
Book title	Publisher		Project title
Other Artwork title/type		Contact information for artist, publisher, or source	
Workshop title		Workshop instructor	

I wish to enter the above item and agree to abide by the quilt contest rules and decisions of the jury and judges. I understand that AQS will take every precaution to protect my quilt exhibited in this show. I realize they cannot be responsible for the acts of nature or others beyond their control. If my quilt is exhibited in the American Quilter's Society Show, I understand that my signature gives AQS the right to use a photo of my quilt for promotion of the AQS Quilt Show in any publications, advertisements, Catalogue of Show Quilts, and other printed or electronic materials. AQS will request permission before using quilts for any other commercial purpose.

_____   _____
Signature   Social Security #

We are proud to present the sponsors for the 20th Anniversary AQS Quilt Show. Each category and event has its own sponsor from the world of quilting. To open the show, the company representatives present the cash awards at the Awards Banquet on Tuesday evening.

Best of Show	Hancock's of Paducah
Hand Workmanship Award	American Quilter's Society
Machine Workmanship Award	Bernina® of America, Inc.
Longarm Machine Quilting Award	Gammill Quilting Machine Company
Workshops/Lectures/Seminars	Pfaff® Sales & Marketing
Fashion Show	AQS, Hobbs Bonded Fibers, Bernina® of America, Inc.
Appliqué, Amateur	Mountain Mist
Appliqué, Professional	Fairfield Processing Corp.
Traditional Pieced, Amateur	Hobbs Bonded Fibers
Traditional Pieced, Professional	Coats & Clark
Mixed Techniques, Amateur	EZ Quilting by Wrights
Mixed Techniques, Professional	Hoffman California Fabrics
Innovative Pieced, Ama. or Prof.	Robert Kaufman Co., Inc.
Group, Amateur or Professional	Mettler Imported by A&E, Inc.
1st Entry in AQS Contest	Morgan Quality Products
Miniature, Amateur or Professional	Benartex, Inc.
Wall, Amateur	FreeSpirit
Wall, Professional	Prym-Dritz Corporation
Pictorial Wall, Amateur or Professional	Husqvarna Viking
Group Wall, Amateur or Professional	C&T Publishing
Judges' Recognition	Possibilities®
Best Wall Quilt	RJR Fabrics
Wall Hand Workmanship Award	McCall's Quilting
Wall Machine Workmanship Award	Brother® International
Sneak Preview Party	Ardco™ by Quiltsmith, Inc.
Teach America 2 Quilt®	Singer®
General Sponsorship	Baby Lock® USA, Elna USA, Koala Cabinets, Nancy's Notions, Optima & O'Lipfa Rulers, Quilting Treasures™, YLI
MAQS Workshop Series	Flynn Quilt Frames, Olfa® Inc. Pfaff® Sales & Marketing
MAQS Monkey Wrench Contest	Clover Needlecraft Inc., Fairfield Processing Corp., Janome America, Inc.
'04 MAQS School Block Challenge	Moda Fabrics